YOUR KNOWLEDGE HAS VALUE

- We will publish your bachelor's and master's thesis, essays and papers

- Your own eBook and book - sold worldwide in all relevant shops

- Earn money with each sale

Upload your text at www.GRIN.com
and publish for free

Bibliographic information published by the German National Library:

The German National Library lists this publication in the National Bibliography; detailed bibliographic data are available on the Internet at http://dnb.dnb.de .

This book is copyright material and must not be copied, reproduced, transferred, distributed, leased, licensed or publicly performed or used in any way except as specifically permitted in writing by the publishers, as allowed under the terms and conditions under which it was purchased or as strictly permitted by applicable copyright law. Any unauthorized distribution or use of this text may be a direct infringement of the author s and publisher s rights and those responsible may be liable in law accordingly.

Imprint:

Copyright © 2013 GRIN Verlag
Print and binding: Books on Demand GmbH, Norderstedt Germany
ISBN: 9783668884267

This book at GRIN:

https://www.grin.com/document/460644

Torsten Eßer

Exclude, accuse, absorb!

Cultural policy-strategies of the Cuban government against rock music, nueva trova, hiphop and reggaeton

GRIN Verlag

GRIN - Your knowledge has value

Since its foundation in 1998, GRIN has specialized in publishing academic texts by students, college teachers and other academics as e-book and printed book. The website www.grin.com is an ideal platform for presenting term papers, final papers, scientific essays, dissertations and specialist books.

Visit us on the internet:

http://www.grin.com/

http://www.facebook.com/grincom

http://www.twitter.com/grin_com

Exclude, accuse, absorb!
Cultural policy-strategies of the Cuban government against rock music, *nueva trova*, hiphop and reggaeton

"The basic clay of our work is the youth;
we place our hope in it and prepare it
to take the banner from our hands."
(Che Guevara)

Abstract:

A few years after the revolution of 1959, jazz (and rock) became identified by Fidel and his friends as „imperialistic music". Though it had never been forbidden to play them, Fidel's „words towards the intellectuals" left enough space to allow some functionaries to ban it from TV- and radio-broadcasting or to hinder the production of discs. A lot of musicians left their island. In case of the *nueva trova*-movement in the mid 60ies at the beginning happened the same as with rock music. But there a new strategy showed more success: embracement, which led to promotion by the government. 30 years later the government – exactly a new and young cultural minister – tried to apply this strategy with the growing hiphop-movement and the reggaeton-scene but failed partly. Many rappers – especially the second generation - did not like to be part of the system. This article compares the different strategies which the Cuban government had used during 50 years to battle against disliked music styles and shows their consequences, successes and failures.

Keywords: Cuba, rockmusic, jazz, nueva trova, hiphop, reggaeton, cultural policy, censorship

In 1959, *los barbudos* – the "bearded", meaning Fidel, Che and their followers – chased the dictator Batista from the country and henceforth put to practice their own political concepts. The state systematically took over control of the cultural life. The new authorities introduced a series of measures which at first did not seem like any structured policies, but which were deemed necessary to satisfy the people's growing demand for culture and were to incorporate, as far as possible, all artists and intellectuals into the revolutionary process. This event had both positive and negative effects for the country's music. The positive effects will be briefly outlined as follows:

- Culture was seen for the first time as a political factor
- Musical institutions, such as orchestras (f.e. National Symphony Orchestra, 1960), music schools and academies, were founded and financially supported by the government (Moore 2006: 80ff)
- Musical education was now free of charge and accessible to (nearly) everyone
- Musicians that were deemed acceptable were given a basic salary by the state
- Manufacturers were established to produce (small) music instruments
- The newly created National Council for Culture – elevated to Ministry of Cultural Affairs in 1976 – developed a national system of festivals for the various forms of music, such as the *Festival Nacional del Son* or the *Festival de Música Electroacústica*, which offered upcoming new talents the opportunity to present themselves to a broader public.
- The research into national folklore was supported, especially in the field of music, by institutions such as the National Museum for Music (1971) and the *Centro de Investigación de Música Cubana*, CIDMUC, founded in 1978 (OEI 2001).

But the focus on supporting national roots in music automatically also led to first signs of suspicion, as musicologist Leonardo Acosta points out: *"Actually, in the first years after the revolution the cultural policy was fairly flexible and open, but there were already a few nationalist traits. Jazz, for example, at the time was generally seen as being imperialistic"* (Interview, Havanna 5/1999).

Politically speaking, the revolution quickly took a stance in opposition to the USA, which, as is generally known, ended in outspoken enmity. This also affected the music, as on the one hand it became more difficult for the musicians to earn money, travel and produce recordings, and on the other hand, what the revolutionaries and party functionaries thought and expected of culture – and specifically of music – was very different from the way democratic politicians dealt with music. *"...se acabó la diversión, llegó el comandante, mandó a parar..."*, these are the lyrics of the revolution's *trovador* Carlos Puebla, taken from the song "*Y en eso llegó Fidel*" – unwittingly, he also describes a development here that was to cause grave problems for the music scene. Indeed, in the course of supporting the national roots, and especially in an attempt to distinguish Cuban music from that of the USA, fairly early on a certain distrust of artists can be made out in Cuba's cultural scene. In 1961, the short documentary film "P.M." was banned. This act of film censorship startled artists and intellectuals, and led to a first major debate on the relationship between culture and politics (Schumann 2001a: 671) There were endless discussions in which Fidel Castro tried to convince the intellectuals of the necessity of the measure taken, and tried to define their relationship to the revolution. The debate eventually culminated in his "Speech to Intellectuals", in which Castro coined what must be his most-quoted postulation: *"Within the Revolution, everything. Against the Revolution, no rights at all!"* (Ministerio de Educación 1986/87: 29). This key sentence of Cuban cultural policies does not contain any specific criteria, nothing enforceable – everything might be prohibited, but many things might also be allowed. And this ambiguity has ever since marked the relationship between the state and various youth cultures and music scenes. Anglo-American expressions and forms of culture as well as music styles were brought into disrepute – the first "victims" being rock music and jazz (Eßer 2004: 41ff).

Midnight Music

Cuban teenagers were enthusiastic about the emerging new rock'n'roll. Bands like the *Hot Rockers* or *Los Llópiz* copied the hits of Elvis Presley and Bill Haley. But it did not take long until this kind of music was no longer featured in the state media. Indeed, the respective artists were not only no longer funded, but they were having to face restrictions concerning their performances or recording requirements (Manduley López 1997: 137ff). Rock music was not discovered to be an *"important factor in political affairs concerning youth and culture,"* as Erich Honecker propounded when he assumed office in the GDR (Rauhut 1999: 32).

A new music style, the *mocambique*, was propagated by the government as an alternative to rock, comparable to LIPSI in the GDR. The idea was to marginalise the American rock music. In the 1960s, things had escalated so far that owning foreign rock LPs could have a negative influence on a young person's CV: for example, they had to face being expelled from school. To the revolutionaries, rock music was cultural imperialism and as such likely to politically and ideologically impregnate society. Though rock music was never officially banned, the musicians' work was often thwarted and lyrics were censored. Ignorance and in part also suppression were the strategies applied for rock music (González Moreno 2004: 309-310). In Cuba, rock came to be known as *musica nocturna* (midnight music), because this was the only time of day when one could listen to rock music relatively unharmed.

History's Paradox: whereas in 1968 hippies and "revolutionaries" in the rest of the world chose Che Guevara to be the icon of their peace movement, the Cuban government would not suffer the few Cuban *jipangos* (hippies) – at best, they were "only" discriminated against, at worst, they were imprisoned. Indeed, from 1968 on, censorship became more drastic, caused amongst other things by the increasing economical dependency of the Soviet Union (Zeuske 2000: 197). Censorship was especially tough during the five "grey" years of 1971 to 1975. It culminated in 1973 in a radio and television broadcast ban for any kinds of Anglo-American music (Manuel 1987: 164). Rauhut's statement concerning the GDR can also be applied to Cuba: *"The aim was to hunt down the class enemy, who seemed never to rest and to even subvert socialism by means of sounds and rhythms"* (Rauhut 1999: 33). This is why the rock music scene stagnated until the 1980s. Finally, in 1981, the first rock festival was staged in Havana, named *"Invierno Caliente"* (Manduley López 1997: 136). However, all the many repressions could not prevent the run of events; the young people simply developed their very own system of strategies to counter these repressions.

Jazz did not really fare much better until the 1980s, it merely had the fortune of very rarely having lyrics that were deemed suspicious and of not engendering a very conspicuous youth culture. But jazz musicians had to suffer just as much from the state's cultural policies. As musicologist Leonardo Acosta explained, *"this was less of one political strategy concerning culture than many different strategies, because ever and again things were suddenly possible that had been prohibited otherwise"* (Interview, Havanna 5/ 1999).

The official stance concerning jazz music only began to relax a little after the mid-1970s, when bands like *Irakere* were internationally successful. *Irakere* won the Grammy Award in 1978 – henceforth, state institutions supported the career of the musicians and accepted foreign currency in exchange. Trumpeter Bobby Carcassés even convinced the functionaries of the fact that jazz music was indeed *"not imperialistic but the music of the suppressed blacks"*, and as such beyond suspicion. He was allowed to organise the first jazz festival in Havana, in 1980 (Interview, Havanna 5/ 1999).

Life became increasingly easier for the *roquéros,* too, from the 1990s on. Today, there are various rock festivals and even an agency, the *Agencia Cubana de Rock,* founded in 2007. Every now and then, CD-productions or single radio or television appearances were allowed, but only for mainstream bands. Heavy metal or death metal bands such as *Z E U S* or *Tendencia*, much coveted by musicians and the audience, were still not given any performance permissions, as the majority were known for their proclivity for provoking:

Rockers are tolerated but still seen as representatives of an inimical counter culture. Some musicians / bands are still frustrated about the political and economical situation. In July 2013, making use of the new freedom to travel, all members of the heavy metal band *Hipnosis* absconded and settled down in the US. It should be pointed out that their life had already been rather privileged, as they had been supported by the *Agencia Cubana de Rock* (Primera 2013a).

Critical lyrics are still punished drastically, as shows the example of the punk-rock band *Porno para Ricardo*. Formed in 1999, this band has been provocative from the outset: Their logo, for example, shows the sickle and hammer in the form of genitals. In their songs, they discuss drugs, prostitution and other social problems, make fun of the

International hymn and deride the system with t-shirt designs sporting prints such as "1959 – the year of delusion". They did not even spare Fidel Castro: *El Comandante* is the title of a song that starts out very harmlessly only to then pour scorn and derision on Castro as the Máximo Líder, really a *Coma Andante,* a walking undead and senile dodderer. It did not take long for the state to react: since 2002, the band has been banned from appearing on stage; lead vocalist Gorki Aguila was later sentenced to two years in prison on charges of possession of toxic substances. Following international complaints, he was released from prison and made to immigrate to Mexico (Gross 2008). It is here that the band is working on a new album, which again will be distributed underhand and online.

Since *Porno para Ricardo* call themselves a punk-rock band, I would like to briefly point out the situation of punks in Cuba, of which there are no more than 100. Most Cubans judge piercings and tattoos as *"mental and social defects"* (Gutiérrez Baró 2002: 59-61), and so Cuban punks are automatically treated as scum. Harlem, whom I interviewed in 2001 in Havana, supported this observation: *"If you look the way we do, most people are first of all very shocked. Some people look at us as if we were exotic animals. The police control us permanently and frequently clap us into prison."* It is true that the German (punk-)rock band *Die Toten Hosen* was invited to play in May 2001 on the occasion of the music fair "Cubadisco" (Eßer 2001: 60), but that was only a minor concession. *"We embody the exact opposite of all that the officials represent and think. To them, we will always remain rebels",* Harlem says. The globally valid motto of punks, "No Future", simply doesn't fit in with the visions of the revolution, die Fidel Castro so formulierte: *"Nosotros tenemos sobre todo, la vista puesta en el futuro, y nosotros tenemos una idea clara de lo que el futuro será"* (Castro 1986/87: 52).

The carrot and the stick

In the 1960s, the government chose a strategy different to the one used concerning rock music for the *nueva trova*. In the early 1960s, the young vocalists such as Pablo Milanés, Silvio Rodríguez, Noel Nicola, Vicente Feliú and others, did not only orientate themselves towards Latin-American models like Atahualpa Yupanqui in Argentina or Violeta Parra and Victor Jara in Chile, but also included inspiration from Bob Dylan or the *The Beatles* in their songs. This fact, and their libertine lyrics, was initially eyed very suspiciously by the officials working for the Ministry for Culture, and so the *nueva trova*-singers were also barely present in the media. Concerts were usually only played in small venues, factory halls or libraries. Only the *Casa de las Américas* supported this movement from the very beginning. It was this institution that put an end to the cultural embargo in July 1967 and hosted the 1. International Protest Song Meeting in Havana, to which songwriters from 16 different countries came (Díaz 1994: 22).

The *Centro de la Canción Protesta,* which existed from 1967 to 1969, helped consolidate the development of the protest song into the political song of Cuba. After the Conference on Education and Culture of 1971, the *trovadores* met with growing governmental acceptance. And finally, in 1972 the movement of the *nueva trova* was founded. This meant both financial support and institutionalisation. *Nueva trova* now became an official term. Suddenly, the singers had access to the mass media and to professional recording studios, which led to a true and proper *nueva trova* euphoria in the mid-1970s (Faya 1995: 359-360). The strategy of "embracement" succeeded: especially young people identified with the modern lyrics. The songs of the Cuban *trovadores* became known beyond the national borders, their representatives were the figureheads of the peoples' fight against oppression and cultural imperialism. Later, Pablo Milanés and Silvio Rodríguez even became members of the Cuban parliament (Eßer 2004: 49).

However, even then, and later, there were still cases of censorship. Singer-songwriter Pedro Luis Ferrer had to endure the ups and downs caused by the mighty state, from refused travel permits and performance bans through to stage appearances in front of thousands of people. Many of his songs were met with suspicion on the side of the state officials, because he used all possible methods of subversion in his lyrics to protest against conditions in Cuba. However, the body of censors often could not read between the lines of these ambiguous texts. In spite of this, he was banned from large-scale public performances in large venues and from coverage in the mass media in 1986 – his songs as such were not prohibited as they were too popular with the people, being passed on as music tapes throughout the island (Franzbach 1999: 8; Schumann 2001a: 291). Today, even the state record shops offer his recordings and he is once more permitted to play in larger venues. Songwriter Carlos Varela had to endure similar experiences: his songs like "Tropicollage" and "*Jalisco Park*" were censored, like his "*Guillermo Tell*" in which he implicitly compared Fidel Castro to William Tell. Nevertheless, meanwhile he too is allowed to travel and release new albums. The popularity of Ferrer and Varela can also be explained by the fact that they formed some sort of opposite pole to 'institutionally approved' singers like Milanés and Rodríguez.

Between censorship and embracement

Hiphop came to Cuba in the late 1980s from Miami, via radio and TV. It bloomed during the *período especial en tiempos de paz* (special period in times of peace) - an euphemism used to express the population's devastating lack of the bare necessities in the early 1990s - because it enabled the young rappers to express their frustration about the two-tier society (with access to US-Dollars or not) that was taking shape at the time. It fared a fate much like rock music had before: in the eyes of the state, Anglo-American music had no rights to existence whatsoever. For the Hiphop community, which had been continuously growing since the late 1980s, there were no possibilities to perform publicly, and of course no access to the recording studios and media, all being run by the government. Yet, self-made tapes with recordings of Cuban rap were circulating everywhere. Because of the general lack of basic equipment, rappers initially used musical backgrounds from the US for their own lyrics. But it did not take long until the predominantly black youth started to produce their own songs, making do with what scarce technology they had, and very often voicing social criticism (Hernández Baguer 2004: 353-345). There came a time when the government realised that this music could no longer be thwarted, so they tried to channel and nationalise it. Henceforth, it had the status of – I quote the ministry of culture – *"an authentic expression of Cuban culture"* (Contreras 2002). Culture secretary Abel Prieto explained too, *"in the past, we had prejudices and we made mistakes, for example concerning rock'n'roll. This is over."* Prieto was an outspoken *Beatles* fan, he was the driving force behind the erection of the John Lennon sculpture which Fidel Castro inaugurated in the year 2000. The cultural fraction of the Communist Youth, the association *Hermanos Saíz*, founded their own rap group, *Grupo Uno,* and in 2002, a state-run agency was founded, the *Agencia Cubana de Rap*, which is still active. From 1995 on, a rap festival was staged in Alamar, on the outskirts of Havana. However, financial support for the handpicked artists (criteria including artistic and political aspects) was so meagre that the movement could not develop into an autonomous force. The rappers also used coded texts to escape censorship, but at the same time their lyrics became less pungent because this was the only chance of being granted a CD production. These musicians had realised that it made more sense to use the state than to stand up against it. Their lyrics still dealt with social deficiencies, but they never criticised Fidel Castro. And so, the *Maximo líder* gave this style of music his blessing, when, in December 1999, he officially received the *Orishas,* a band who in the meantime was living in Paris. But even in 1997, when the band *Primera Base* recorded their first CD, the situation must already have relaxed somewhat, or else how could they have sung about a *"Jinetera",* a prostitute, since these were officially non-existent? (Foehr 2001: 38-41)

The rise of reggaetón, as well as tension within the hiphop scene and with the government institutions finally led to the abortion of the only official hiphop festival in 2005 and to a general weakening of that music scene, though there was a short revival in 2007, brought about by the success of the hiphop duo *Los Aldeanos*. But due to their lyrics and severe antirevolutionary statements published by international media, the duo was banned in mid-2009 from any further public performances, which also meant that the entire hiphop scene suffered from this denigration (Baker 2011: 357-358). Although the sanctions were revoked in 2010, even a governmental "rehabilitation" of hiphop could not revive this movement, as some media follow their own ideas and still prefer to more or less ignore this music. Today, less rap music is being produced although – thanks to the widespread new technologies like Internet, mp3 etc. – there is a wider audience, both national and international. Nowadays, Cuban hiphop is simply seen as one music style amongst many others – a turn of fate that might also await reggaetón, although it must be pointed out that state-of-the-art technology allows much better quality (Baker 2011: 354-356).

Reggaetón is the most popular music style amongst Cuba's urban youth. It was developed in the 1990s in Puerto Rico and Panama, and at the beginning of the new millennium it became a world-wide success. Reggaetón is a mixture of Jamaican reggae, rap-vocals, house rhythms and various Caribbean styles. The largely simple, macho lyrics and the respective explicitly sexual dance style fit in very smoothly with the prevailing machismo culture. Bands such as *Maxima Alerta* and *Klan Destino,* from Santiago de Cuba, or *Candyman* draw thousands of fans to their concerts (González Bello et al. 2006: 3-5/ 8-9).

The state has long since disapproved of the sexist lyrics and body moves, but they were tolerated because of their success and the foreign currency they brought. But this tolerance has reached its limit now: early 2013, various high functionaries, amongst others Orlando Vistel, president of the "Cuban Institute for Music", scorned reggaetón as "vulgar, banal and misogynistic". Consequently, this music has been banned from the media, from public buildings and outdoor spaces, which – in view of the many street parties – is seen as the worst measure of all (Henkel 2013; Manrique 2012). This is a retreat into old strategies, which are rather useless if we consider the possibilities offered by new technology nowadays, and it comes just a few months after the abolishment of a blacklist – never officially authorised – of about 50 artists (such as Celia Cruz, Paquito D'Rivera, Willy Chirino) who had been banned from the radio (Rainsford 2012).

Conclusion

Cuba's cultural political strategies have on the whole become more tolerant since the 1990's, in spite of the odd relapse into olden days. This is mainly due to the fact that media such as satellite TV and Internet circumvent any form of censorship. The Cuban youth, aged 14-30, who constitute approximately 25% of the population, are appeased by guest performances of international bands such as the *Manic Street Preachers* (2003) or *Calle 13* (2010). 2009 saw the staging of the music festival "Paz sin Fronteras", starring Juanes, Victor Manuel and others in front of an audience exceeding one million people (Vicent 2009). But most steps taken by the state did not lead to the intended results – as can be seen by a short glance into the *calle* G in Havana's centre on a Friday night: up to 2,000 young people gather here – rockers, punks, hiphoppers, emos – grouped according to their affiliation, and suspiciously eyed by the state officials. Again and again, the government reverts to old reflexes. This applies to rock musicians as much as, most recently, to jazz musician Roberto Carcassés, who had championed free elections during a concert and was to be sanctioned afterwards – only Silvio Rodríguez's intervention could prevent this (Primera 2013b). Concerning the young people in a (post-socialist) future Cuba, they will most likely experience what happened in the former communist countries after the fall of the Berlin Wall: individualisation processes in society as well as the influence of globalisation on the economy, on politics and on culture will change the traditional social forms such as family, associations, political parties and so forth. This, in turn, will foster the development of a wide and uncontrollable range of youth cultures. The outcome is what Richard Sennett calls "flexible man" with a chameleon-like changeable personality and without any long-term bonds. In contrast, Che Guevara's "New Man", someone who commits himself selflessly and without any material interest to the common good, even sacrificing himself if need be, will remain a utopian vision for Cuba, too (Eßer 2011: 62).

Table: Actions and consequences of cuban cultural policy-strategies

	Rock	Jazz	Nueva Trova	Hiphop/ Reggaetón	Punk
reasons for dislike	- music of the imperialistic enemy (US) - critical texts	- music of the imperialistic enemy (US)	- critical texts	- music of the imperialistic enemy (US) - critical texts / - bawdy texts and dance	- texts - look - provocation
governmental strategy	- repression - toleration	- repression - toleration - promotion	- criticism - embracement - promotion	Hiphop: - repression - embracement / Reggaetón: - toleration - repression	- repression
governmental actions	- no financial contributions - no media exposure - obstruction of (public) performances - censorship of texts - discrimination of musicians and fans - jail	- no financial contributions - rarely media exposure - obstruction of (public) performances	- rarely media exposure at the beginnig - discrimination of musicians - obstruction of (public) performances	- rarely media exposure at the beginnig - no financial contributions - censorship of texts - obstruction of (public) performances	- no financial contributions - no media exposure - permanent street controls - jail
consequences	- small scene - circulation of ilegal tapes - preference of extreme styles of rockmusic (Metal, Dark) as rebellion - musicians went into exile - but also partly adaptation	- musicians went into exile - musicians changed genre	- circulation of ilegal tapes - musicians went into exile - but also partly adaptation	- circulation of ilegal tapes - production with US-american backgrounds - but also partly adaptation	- tiny scene (ca. 100)
counter-actions of musicians / fans	- concerts at „secret" locations - undermine censorship with coded texts - stamina - smuggle material into	- conviction of functionaires that jazz is the music of depressed blacks in the US. afterwards 1.	- concerts at „secret" locations - undermine censorship with coded texts	- concerts at „secret" locations - undermine censorship with coded texts - smuggle material into the internet	- concerts at „secret" locations

	the internet	jazzfestival			
current situation	the rock music scene alternates between repression, promotion and resignation	jazz is accepted and promoted	trova is accepted and promoted	hiphop is accepted and little promoted / reggaetón currently is repressed	punk is officially not existent

Bibliography

Baker, Geoffrey (2011), *Buena Vista in the club. Rap, reggaetón, and revolution in Havana*, Durham and London, Duke University Press.

Castro, Fidel (1998), *Fidel habla a la juventud: selección 1960-1998*, La Habana, Casa Ed. Abril.

Contreras, Joseph (2002), "Hip-Hopping in Havana", *Newsweek*, 13.5.

Díaz, Clara (1994), *La nueva trova,* La Habana, Letras Cubanas.

Eßer, Torsten (2011), „'No future'? Jugend- und Musikszenen im Kreuzfeuer kubanischer Kulturpolitik", *Hispanorama* Nr. 132, p. 54-62.

Eßer, Torsten (2004), „Sozialismus mit Rhythmus. Kubanische Kulturpolitik seit 1959 und ihre Auswirkungen auf die Musik", in: Eßer, Torsten/ Patrick Frölicher (eds.), *Alles in meinem Dasein ist Musik... Kubanische Musik von Rumba bis Techno*, Frankfurt a.M., Vervuert, p. 33-74.

Eßer, Torsten (2001), "Kein Opium für Fidel. Die Toten Hosen in Havanna", *Matices* Nr. 30, p. 60-61.

Faya, Alberto (1995), "Nueva trova y cultura de la rebeldía", in: Giro, Radamés (ed.), *Panorama de la música popular cubana*, La Habana, Letras Cubanas, p. 351-361.

Foehr, Stephen (2001), *Waking up in Cuba,* London, Santuary Publishing.

Franzbach, Martin (1999), "Das politische Lied als poetische Waffe in Kuba", *IKA Zeitschrift für Internationalen Kulturaustausch* 58, p. 6-9.

González Bello, Neris/ Liliana Casanella Cué/ Grizel Hernández Baguer (2006), *El reguetón en Cuba. Un análisis de sus particularidades,* Actas del VII Congreso IASPM-AL, La Habana.

González Moreno, Liliana (2004), „Subversiv wider Willen. Rockmusik auf Kuba", in: Eßer, Torsten/ Patrick Frölicher (eds.), *Alles in meinem Dasein ist Musik... Kubanische Musik von Rumba bis Techno*, Frankfurt a.M., Vervuert, p. 307-324.

Gross, Thomas (2008), „Mit Punk gegen den Comandante", *DIE ZEIT*, 23.12.

Gutiérrez Baró, Elsa (2002), *Muy en serio y algo en broma: diálogo con los adolescentes*, La Habana, Ed. Científico-Técnica.

Henkel, Knut (2013), "Die Obszönität der Krise. Zensur gegen Cubatón", *Neue Züricher Zeitung*, 8.3.

Hernández Baguer, Grizel/ Liliana Casanella Cué (2004), "Eine spannungsgeladene Beziehung. Die Revolution und der Rap", in: Eßer, Torsten/ Patrick Frölicher (eds.), *Alles in meinem Dasein ist Musik... Kubanische Musik von Rumba bis Techno*, Frankfurt a.M., Vervuert, p. 353-363.

Manduley López, Humberto (1997), "Rock in Cuba: History of a wayward son", *The South Atlantic Quarterly* 96.1, p. 135-141.

Manrique, Diego A (2012), „Cuba quiere acabar con el ‚perreo'", *El País*, 21.12.

Manuel, Peter (1987), "Marxism, nationalism and popular music in revolutionary Cuba", *Popular Music* 6.2, p. 161-178.

Ministerio de Educación (ed.) (1986/87), *Pensamiento y política cultural cubanos* (tomos I-IV), La Habana, Pueblo y Educación.

Moore, Robin D. (2006), *Music & Revolution. Cultural Change in Socialist Cuba*, Los Angeles, University of California Press.

OEI (Organización de Estados Iberoamericanos para la Educación, la Ciencia y la Cultura) (2001), *Sistemas nacionales de cultura: Informe Cuba*, CD-ROM, Madrid.

Primera, Maye (2013a), "A Miami con toda la banda", *El País*, 8.8.

Primera, Maye (2013b), "Castigo y perdón para un músico cubano", *El País*, 19.9.

Rainsford, Sarah (2012), "Cuba's ban on anti-Castro musicians quietly lifted", *BBC News online*, 8.8.

Rauhut, Michael (1999), "Rockmusik in der DDR. Politische Koordinaten und alltägliche Dimensionen", *Aus Politik und Zeitgeschichte* Nr. 28, p. 32-38.

Schumann, Peter B. (2001a), "Dissident in Kuba–Formen politischer und kultureller Opposition", in: Ette, Ottmar/Franzbach, Martin (eds.), *Kuba heute*, Frankfurt a.M., Vervuert, p. 291-309.

Schumann, Peter B (2001b), "Der kubanische Film im Kontext der Kulturpolitik", in: Ette, Ottmar/Franzbach, Martin (eds.), *Kuba heute*, Frankfurt a.M., Vervuert, p. 669-682.

Vicent, Mauricio (2009), „Primero el ritmo, luego la política", *El País*, 21.9.

Zeuske, Michael (2000), *Kleine Geschichte Kubas*, München, Beck.

Biography

Torsten Eßer (*1966), author, editor (radio) and freelance-journalist, Cologne, ASPM-member. He gives lectures and publishes books, articles and reviews in books and scientific magazines, radio-and TV-programms, mainly about latin american and spanish culture, music and politics, f.e.: (Eds., with Patrick Frölicher) *„Alles in meinem Dasein ist Musik...". Kubanische Musik von Rumba bis Techno*, Vervuert, Frankfurt 2004/ (with Walther L. Bernecker and Peter Kraus) *Kleine Geschichte Kataloniens*, Suhrkamp, Frankfurt 2007 (www.torstenesser.de).

YOUR KNOWLEDGE HAS VALUE

- We will publish your bachelor's and master's thesis, essays and papers

- Your own eBook and book -
  sold worldwide in all relevant shops

- Earn money with each sale

Upload your text at www.GRIN.com
and publish for free